The Stories
of Raymond Carver

The Stories of Raymond Carver

A CRITICAL STUDY

Kirk Nesset

Ohio University Press
Athens

Ohio University Press, Athens, Ohio 45701
© 1995 by Kirk Nesset
Printed in the United States of America
All rights reserved
07 06 05 04 03 02 01 00   6 5 4
Ohio University Press books are printed on acid-free paper ∞

Library of Congress Cataloging-in-Publication Data
Nesset, Kirk.
    The stories of Raymond Carver : a critical study / Kirk Nesset.
        p.   cm.
    Includes bibliographical references (p.   ) and index.
    ISBN 0-8214-1099-7 (cloth). — ISBN 0-8214-1100-4 (paperback)
    1. Carver, Raymond—Criticism and interpretation.
2. Postmodernism (Literature)—United States.   3. Realism in
literature.   4. Short story.   I. Title.
PS3553.A7894Z78   1994
813'.54—dc20   94-30322
                                                                    CIP

For V. V.

Contents

Acknowledgements

ABOVE ALL I OWE THANKS here to William Stull, Carver's bibliographer and foremost champion, not only for the many fine books and essays he has published by and about Carver but also for his willingness to correspond on these matters — for the many letters and phone calls we exchanged, for his generosity and unwavering patience, and for that fine Vietnamese meal back in Hartford. I am also grateful to Tess Gallagher, whose blessing means very much to me, and whose comments were invaluable to this project (chapter 4 in particular). Thanks are due, too, to Steven Allaback, for his good judgment and honesty, and for the use of his refuge one summer, his sunny house by the sea. I am thankful as well to Steven Jensen for his sharp editorial eye, and to Pam Hengst at Whittier College, for all her secretarial help. Finally, I am indebted to the editors of *American Literature*, *Essays in Literature*, and *Profils Americains*, both for publishing chapters of this manuscript (or parts of chapters, some in slightly different form) and for their permission to reprint that material here.

K. N.

Introduction

RAYMOND CARVER WAS BORN IN 1938 in Clatskanie, Oregon, a small sawmill town near the Columbia River. After graduating from high school he worked at the mill with his father (a hard drinking laborer who had migrated west from Arkansas), married shortly after his nineteenth birthday, and had two children within the first eighteen months of his marriage. Carver moved to California in 1958 and enrolled at Chico State College, where, pressed by financial worries, he worked "crap jobs," as he called them, to support his family. Two years later he transferred to Humboldt State College to finish his degree, during which time he began publishing his first poems and stories in little magazines. By the early seventies his literary reputation had grown to the extent that he began accepting visiting appointments at universities, although as a result of his drinking — which worsened steadily in the seventies, and nearly killed him before he gave it up in 1977 — his early teaching career was anything but ideal.

The nature of Carver's success — his meteoric rise to international acclaim, his widespread appeal, his continuing influence on American letters — seems all the more extraordinary in light of such inauspicious beginnings. Between 1976 and 1988 he published ten books of poetry and prose, as well as numerous chapbooks and limited editions. An eleventh book, another collection of poems, appeared in 1989, the year after he died. He was the recipient of many awards, including a Guggenheim Fellowship, Poetry magazine's Levinson Prize, a National Book Circle Critics Award, the prestigious Mildred and Harold Strauss Living Award, nominations for the Pulitzer Prize, and an honorary Doctorate of Letters from

Hartford University. Among other things, Carver has been dubbed the rejuvenator of the dying American short story, the godfather of literary "minimalism," and in light of recent trends in American writing, the most imitated American writer since Hemingway.

Despite the happy circumstances of the final decade of Carver's life, however — despite literary recognition, despite his victory over alcohol, and, after a trying divorce, his fortuitous linking with and marriage to writer Tess Gallagher — his work continued to reflect the difficult circumstances of his former life. From the earliest story to the last, Carver's characters are unhappily estranged, out of work, disillusioned by meaningless jobs and meaningless marriages; they suffer in various degrees from alcoholism as well as bad luck and bad timing, battered by a world which typically leaves them inert and speechless in the wake of longings and fears they cannot begin to identify. The "trademark Carver tale," one critic writes, "is a kind of mundane ghost story in which . . . people are haunted by the presence of some lost, almost forgotten, not-really-expected possibility." [1] Alienated from ideals and aspirations they only dimly comprehend, and ultimately from themselves, Carver's figures play out, in the words of another critic, "the terrifying implications of Normal Life." Dreading the approach of the bill collector, knocked down by marital infidelity or the torments of delirium tremens, they live out "normal nightmares" from which they rarely awake. [2] And yet while such scenarios reflect to an extent the darkest periods of Carver's early married life, they also attest to his triumph, to that miraculous recovery of sorts, and to Carver's uncanny capacity for transforming life into art, for erecting a monument to pain even as he learned to transcend it.

Unique as the stories are in subject and manner, one need not look far to see how securely Carver's fiction is rooted in a recognizable literary tradition. With elliptical spareness and precision, alive with repetition though flattened by his characteristic deadpan tone, Carver's prose hearkens back obviously to Hemingway (with an important distinction concerning voice: as Jay McInerney observes, Carver has dispensed with the "romantic egoism" which makes the "Hemingway idiom such an awkward model for other writers in the late 20th century"). [3] Carver's style — starkly terse, vibrating with unspoken energies of indecision, dread and half-hearted expectation, modulating in mood from darkly humorous to

grim to positively eerie — also draws notably from Kafka, whose uncanny moods are evoked in the coupling of hyper-rational prose with sur-
real, irrational scenarios and events. Carver's subjects, in similar fashion,
place him squarely in a tradition of American prose writing, fixing him at
the end of a trajectory extending from Sherwood Anderson to John
O'Hara to John Cheever, and mirroring another trajectory, a Russian one,
extending from Turgenev to Chekov, writers in whom Carver was in-
tensely interested. Carver's subjects, in other words, are aligned with
those of authors who have for decades given voice to the woes and disen-
chantments of modern (industrial, urban, suburban) life. Cheever,
Carver's immediate predecessor — whom Carver befriended in Iowa
(employed briefly as teachers, the two enjoyed days-long drinking binges
together) — made a living recapitulating this obsession, giving voice to
the enchantment of American disenchantment. Cheever perhaps summed
it up best in "The Death of Justina":

There are some Americans who, although their fathers emigrated from the Old
World three centuries ago, never seem to have quite completed the voyage and I am
one of these. I stand, figuratively, with one wet foot on Plymouth Rock, looking
with some delicacy, not into a formidable and challenging wilderness but onto a
half-finished civilization embracing glass towers, oil derricks, suburban continents,
and abandoned movie houses and wondering why, in this most prosperous, equi-
table, and accomplished world — where even the cleaning women practice the
Chopin preludes in their spare time — everyone should seem to be disappointed.[4]

Hovering near the end of this continuum of dashed hopes and disillu-
sionment, Carver's characters are noticeably more disappointed than
Cheever's. Given the severity of their predicaments and their limited powers of apprehension, they tend to lack both the capacity and the impetus
necessary for the task of "wondering why." Springing in turn from
Anderson's "grotesques" and Cheever's unhappy suburbanites, Carver's
figures take American disappointment to its barest extreme, haunted as
they are by unfulfillable, intangible longings, paralyzed, lost, pushed well
beyond the verge of articulate dismay. Unlike Cheever's characters,
Carver's cannot speak their pain. They translate it instead into obsessive
behavior, into desperate and abusive patterns, into drinking, smoking,
and eating, into adultery, into voyeurism and, on occasion, violence —

bitterly though humorously calls a "tragedy," and in the course of the story he makes overtures toward reestablishing a focus in his life — the focus to which the story's title gives play. Thus he bids his guest take multiple photographs — photographs suggesting stasis, aptly enough, in the sense of both frozen space and time and of familial unity (portraits of family and home). Slightly more self-aware if also more detached and cynical than his predecessors, this speaker seeks himself in the viewfinder, personal stability in a destablized world. Yet in keeping with Carver's dark view of things, stability is no mere stone's throw away. "I don't do motion shots," the photographer shouts as his host hurls rocks from the roof, implying that his host may emerge in the developed photos only as the emotional blur he is at present, and perhaps has been much of his life. "It won't work," the photographer warns him early on, intuiting the circumstances: "They're not coming back." Similarly in a later story, "Vitamins," a deranged veteran named Nelson admonishes a young couple who are bewildered by their lives and who seek emotional nutrients in the compensatory way of sex. "It ain't going to do no good!" Nelson yells, echoing the man with the hooks, though even more strangely prophetic in tone and bearing; his words are indeed a hard pill to swallow: "Whatever you do, it ain't going to help none!"[10]

Heaving stones into the air and shouting, the abandoned husband of "Viewfinder" is one of a number of male characters in *What We Talk About When We Talk About Love* overcome by violence in their personal frustrations. One hurls a jar of pickles through a window while another sabotages fresh-baked pies and slashes the cord on the phone. One kills his wife with a hammer; another cudgels a pair of young women to death with a rock. Rising out of the fear and paranoia of *Will You Please Be Quiet, Please?* and mellowing later into the relative placidity of *Cathedral*, these outbursts attest to the inevitable course of buried violence in Carver's world — to the return of the repressed, and to the extremity at the heart of all conflict, and of all stories, be the violence readily visible or not. But there is more to the escapade on the roof in "Viewfinder" than the uncorking of bottled frustration and anger, which is mild here in comparison to that in other stories. It is as much an act of exhibitionism as it is an emotional vent (the photographer, understandably embarrassed, responds by checking "up and down the street"), and not unrelated to the am-

putee's parading of his hooks. Carver's frantic lovers and ex-lovers display
their problems to the world in order to externalize those problems, ad-
vertising their grief as a kind of emotional last resort. In "Will You
Please Be Quiet, Please?" for instance, Ralph tells a roomful of complete
strangers in a bar about his wife's infidelity. In "Menudo" a despondent
Hughes goes from yard to yard raking lawns, dramatizing the extent of
his despair while the neighborhood looks on. In "Why Don't You
Dance?" an abandoned husband sets a whole houseful of furniture out
onto his lawn, fully and unabashedly placing the intimate details of his
ruined private life in plain view of the public. Exhibitionism, in all of
these cases, is a last-ditch attempt at control where control no longer exists, a means for hurling oneself voluntarily into the thick of misfortune,
rather than being pulled forcibly down.

If vicariousness is one form of self-denial, then exhibitionism is another, which denies self by bowling it over with an image. (For Carver's
lovers, the image is typically one of numbed, restrained desperation.) In
Carver's world, both manifestations seem strangely necessary, serving as
safety valves for characters who struggle along even as — or because —
they deny themselves further, sidestepping confrontations with their
own tenuous, precariously held together identities. And just as such denial takes place in the minds of characters, so is it replicated in Carver's
narratives, and in the overall narrative energies of "Viewfinder." Buried in
the story of the narrator's afternoon with the photographer is another
story, the tale of the narrator's split with his family (and buried also is the
tale of how the man with the hooks lost his hands, which he says is "another story"). The details of the narrator's loss are initially witheld,
emerging only in the scattered intuitions of the guest, unconfirmed until
the story is nearly over. ("The whole kit and kaboodle," the narrator
finally admits, climbing up to the roof. "They cleared right out.") On a
par with the rhetorical politics of the photographer, who smiles at his
host "as if he knew something he wasn't going to tell," the narrator's
politics involve keeping quiet about his misfortunes — for as long as he
can, anyway. By witholding information, the story itself recapitulates the
denial of the denier and, in a deeper sense, his pain. As narrative,
"Viewfinder" embodies and dramatizes rhetorically the subject it sets
forth to tell.

This is really nothing new in top-notch prose fiction — *The Sun Also Rises* comes immediately to mind, with all its deferrals and displacements, Jake's strategies for dealing with his "wound." But Carver has distilled the process, sharpening and tightening, withholding, taking out even more in order to add to the underside of his iceberg. The complicity of rhetorical performance and subject matter also operates naturally on the level of diction, and for this reason Carver's work is often as misunderstood as it is. In tone, "Viewfinder" is characterized by its detachment, by sympathetic, humorous terseness, by an odd verbal hardness which spotlights language as denial itself. Evoking the hard-boiled mind of its speaker, the story's tone embodies tensions between detachment and sympathy, humor and emotional pain, and plays out such tensions on the level of diction and syntax. In one of his most memorable lines, the narrator, referring to his guest's artificial hands, says, "I took a good look at those hooks." In playful Skelton-like fashion half of the words in the sentence rhyme, tempering the final word and focal point of the sentence, "hooks" — itself a small glint of linguistic horror — making catastrophe seem strangely funny. Thus do we displace our own inner turmoil through the visible turmoils of others, Carver's language seems to suggest.

On the microscopic level the story is bursting with such nuances. "Again! I screamed," the story's final sentence reads, "and took up another rock." At this moment, the only real violent one in the story, violence is evoked with sudden fury on the level of language. By far the strongest verb in an otherwise restrained verbal performance, "screamed" constitutes an explosion coinciding with an emotional release. Among other such nuances is Carver's perhaps unintentional revision of Hemingway's use of the term "good." After undergoing an elaborate procedure to climb onto the roof, the speaker finds himself standing atop his house at last, and says, "It was okay up there on the roof." Revising Hemingway's motto "It was good" — applied with incantatory repetition in Nick Adams' healing retreats into the wilderness — the abandoned husband's statement suggests in one small, ordinary word that for Carver the romantic core at the center of Hemingway's modernist vocabulary is now officially dead. We may indeed have to settle for "okay," Carver implies; some of us have never known anything else, if we have been even that lucky. Recovery may not, all things considered, be as plausible a notion as it used to be. "'Ready?'" the narrator calls out from the roof, rock in hand, waiting as the man below steadies his image in the viewfinder. "'Okay!'" the man with the hooks calls back, a response that, for all its seeming simplicity, its minimality, hits exactly the right note.

In 1981, the year *What We Talk About When We Talk About Love* appeared, Carver published, "On Writing," his only essay on the mechanics of fiction. Explaining his predilection for short stories that afford "some feeling of threat or a sense of menace," he writes:

What creates tension in a piece of fiction is partly the way the concrete words are linked together to make up the visible action of the story. But it's also the things that are left out, that are implied, the landscape just under the smooth (but sometimes broken and unsettled) surface of things. [11]

In "Viewfinder," such a "landscape" exists as the buried matter of one man's "tragedy," which though largely "left out" emerges gradually in scattered pieces, if only as a series of hints. In "Why Don't You Dance?," on the contrary, the buried matter of another's man all but identical tragedy never surfaces at all. Noticeably more radical in its suppression of detail, this story leaves the reader to surmise about its central character, a man who has inexplicably set his furniture and household items, even his lamps and stereo, on the lawn and driveway in front of his house. [12] Surveying the residual objects of his former married life, we assume that here is another of Carver's survivors, one more exhibitionistic than most; we assume, too, that like the cars passing by, full of staring onlookers that don't stop, "he [won't], either" — that he will survive in his own, however peculiar, way. As in "Viewfinder," the desperation and emotional denial of the man is underscored by the operations of narrative, mainly by omission and deferral, and by the story's diction, complicit as it is in evoking the minds of its figures.

In "Why Don't You Dance?," Carver's prose is even more terse and detached, so cool and rock-hard, so deliberately flat, that it comes across, as a reviewer says of the book's style in general, "as sparingly clear as a fifth of iced Smirnoff." [13] Operating in the omniscient perspective, the rhetoric of this story evokes here more than anywhere else the chilly, hardened state of its protagonist's mind, and does so relentlessly, beginning with an extensive survey of the man's belongings outside on the driveway and lawn; the cool blankness of the description, in all its inventorying factuality, reflects the emotional denial of the objects' owner, who had until recently viewed the objects as shared property. The voice of the story, in other words, infected by the consciousness of its central figure, reflects and enhances a sense of the man's bitterness and cynicism. Thus the unseen narrator oddly mimics himself (or herself) in describing the objects that once occupied customary sides in the bedroom ("His side, her side"); thus he or she later takes on the emotional resonances of the man, when the "preposterous question" of money comes up regarding the desk.

One of the first things his guests do when they arrive is flop down on the bed — ironically a place that was reserved in former times for the greatest intimacies, and which is now reduced to the kind of lurid public display we have seen elsewhere, a flaunting of intimacy long dead and gone. Lying on the man's bed, dancing to his records in the driveway, the young couple provides both an outlet through which the man may displace his denial (as the photographer does for his host in "Viewfinder") and a living refiguration of his marriage in its infancy, the memory of which he is now attempting to cast off. The nuances of such refiguration, accordingly, come across in the submerged tensions of the couple's conversation, not to mention in the flinty hardness of the prose:

> "How is it?" he said.
> "Try it," she said.
> He looked around. The house was dark.
> "I feel funny," he said. "Better see if anybody's home."
> She bounced on the bed.
> "Try it first," she said.
> He lay down on the bed and put the pillow under his head.
> "How does it feel?" she said.
> "It feels firm," he said.
> She turned on her side and put her hand to his face.
> "Kiss me," she said.
> "Let's get up," he said.
> "Kiss me," she said.

She closed her eyes. She held him.
He said, "I'll see if anybody's home." (5)

In the most obvious sense, the boy and girl are symbolic stand-ins for the couple who bought the bed and shared it before. Less obviously, their conversation betrays tensions in their own relationship, hinting at tensions which may or may not have precipitated the break up of the older couple — most visible in the girl's eager sexual overtures and in the boy's reluctance to act in a potentially embarrassing way. The tensions here, filling the interstices of a conversation they conduct lying down, of all places, on a bed, are grounded in sexual politics. The swelling of the girl's aggressiveness — evidenced more concretely later as she interrupts her boyfriend to bargain with the man, and as she asks the man to dance — suggests that her host's present circumstances (due, perhaps, to a headstrong wife and his own stubbornness) may be a preview of the young couple later on, long after they have acquired the unhappy articles of this man's marriage.

Less obviously yet, the mechanics of the dialogue take these suggestions to an extreme. In this one half-page exchange on the bed, Carver employs sixteen pronouns — most of them forms of "he said" and "she said" — carrying to extremity what has come to be considered a trademark (and much imitated) aspect of his craft. On the most rudimentary level, such narratorial markers serve as deft rhetorical jabs, disrupting with almost irritating consistency the natural rhythm of voice and breath, thus undercutting the traditionally "poetic" potential of what in Carver's ecosystem of down-and-outers are sometimes terribly unpoetic scenes. Further, the rhetorical insistence of "he said" and "she said" also underlines the event of speech and its shortcomings, a major concern in all of Carver's books, particularly this one. It draws still further attention to the act of narration — to the way that the unique post-postmodern brand of alienation Carver's characters suffer also informs his narratives (a subject for another investigation altogether). Most important, however, these markers are assertions of personal identity — or, better, are deliberately awkward gestures in that direction. In the course of the story we learn nothing of the young couple; we are ignorant of who they are, of what they dream about and where they are going. Coupled with such noninformation, the repeated assertions of identity coming in the form of pronouns promote nonidentity more than they do identity, much less full or stable selves. Thus Carver's dance of the pronouns, a curious kind of club-foot shuffle, plays out on the level of language an identity crisis embodied metaphorically in the machinations of his central figure (who is much more a cypher than either one of the kids). "We thought nobody was here," the boy explains awkwardly when the man arrives, his words ringing with more truth than he can imagine. Pulling out his checkbook to pay for the items he buys, the boy says, "I'm making it out to cash," unwittingly equating his host with the monetary worth of his domestic goods, the accumulated baggage of a life that the man now deems utterly and irreversibly worthless.

In the final brief segment of this frayed narrative (a narrative composed of the mutually intertwining perspectives of the man and the young couple), the story favors the girl as it had earlier favored the man. With this shift in perspective, a final comment provides us with something new: a confirmation of the man's worthlessness, now through the eyes of the girl. We are obliged to consider retroactively the narrator's comments about the young couple's expressions, the looks on their faces after they've bargained with him. "It was nice or it was nasty," the man says early on. "There was no telling." They are indeed "nice" kids, the story seems to suggest, and yet they are also eager to exploit circumstances, like vultures carrying off pieces of a dead animal, fattening on disaster. While the girl lacks the intuitive powers of the photographer in "Viewfinder" — she hasn't experienced much yet in the way of hard knocks — she is nevertheless vaguely sensitive to the man's desperation: twice she refers to him as "desperate," the second utterance taking on a more informed aura. Like the waitress in "Fat," she is attuned to concerns that, though larger than her own understanding, seem to apply directly to herself. She likewise voices her concerns, trying to articulate the connection, to "get it all talked out."

In the end, then, the man's story is her story as well as a story about the man, herself, and the boy — one that heightens our sense of both "nasty" insensitivity and nicer curiosity, of exploitation and awkward sympathy, and of the way forebodings can spell out emotional wreckage to come. Appropriately, the wild card in the shuffle of final details Carver lays on the table takes the form of the "record-player" the man gives his guests, along with the "crappy records," as the girl describes them. Innocuous as it might at first seem, this small detail zeroes in on the central concerns of the story: the fathomless nature of the man's bitterness, for all his restraint, and the sorry shallowness of the boy and girl. In a last-minute flourish we are given back a detail which, as in all good, threatening stories, had been withheld. With such flourishes, as one reviewer puts it, Carver ultimately "keeps more than he abandons."[14] As a result we come away from this and other stories not so much with ready meanings but with lessons in reading. Encouraged to look deeply into the stories of others, we learn to read our own more fully and carefully, sidestepping calamities of the future if we can, or at least steeling ourselves for what we cannot avoid.

The fullest story in the collection, ironically, is a story about a man incapable of speech. "The Third Thing That Killed My Father Off" is about what "the wrong kind of women can do to you," to use the words of the narrator's father. But unlike "Viewfinder" and "Why Don't You Dance?" which explore the aftermath of such interactions, this story charts the course of a man's undoing, step by step. Worse off than many of Carver's lot, the story's central figure lacks both a name — Dummy being his nickname — and the capacity for normal self-expression. Unable to articulate himself in conventional ways, unable to get things "talked out," Dummy displaces his concerns, chief among them his fears of his wife's infidelity. He stocks a pond with black bass, and keeps vigil over the fish as he cannot seem to do with his wife. Dummy's fishpond, and the electric fence that surrounds it, is yet another manifestation of the exhibitionist impulse in Carver's world. The exhibition ends, thanks to the return of the repressed and a hammer, with Dummy murdering his wife, and with the spectacle of Dummy himself, suicidally drowned and later fished from his pond (where fishing, humorously enough, is strictly forbidden).

As with other stories, "The Third Thing" relies for much of its rhetorical power on strategies mirrored in the events and details of the story. Like "Sacks," "The Calm," and "Everything Stuck to Him" in this volume, and like "Where I'm Calling From" in the next, "The Third Thing" is a frame tale utilizing several narrative layers. Such layers displace the central impact of the story, much in the way Dummy displaces anger about his wife — anger altogether unarticulated in "Dance," restrained until the end in "Viewfinder," and exploding in this story with unusual energy and violence. Simultaneously encompassing three independent sets of concerns, "The Third Thing" is as much the narrator's story, and the narrator's father's story, as it is Dummy's; the narrative layers intersect thematically, linked by strands of the immediate tale, in which Dummy figures as primary.

"From what I hear," one of Jack's father's friends says, referring to Dummy's new fish and the precautions he takes to protect them, "he'd do better to put that fence round his house." Dummy, however, devotes more and more of himself to the pond, in the course of the story, trying in his own way to "husband" nature, which proves impossible with the coming of heavy rains. (The river, it is worth noting, is distinctly female in its intractability and uncontrollability: "She's up to fifteen feet," Jack's father says of the flooding river, monitoring her rise in the newspaper; in one version of the story — entitled "Dummy," appearing four years earlier in *Furious Seasons* — the river is referred to in the same sentence as "it's.") [15] Among other things, Dummy's tale is about the futility of trying to control the uncontrollable, and about the ways one compensates for failure, an issue mirrored in the tale of Jack's father, within which it is immediately framed.

"I'll tell you what did my father in," Jack says in the first sentence of the story. "The third thing was Dummy, that Dummy died. The first thing was Pearl Harbor. And the second thing was moving to my grandfather's farm near Wenatchee. That's where my father finished out his days, except they were probably finished out before that." Like Dummy, Jack's father knows disorder: he has seen it manifested in his life most recently in the form of a murdering, suicidal friend, and earlier in a threat to national security (a surprise attack) and in his necessary acceptance of poverty's strictures, prompted as he was to move home as a middle-aged man. Jumbling the symptoms of his father's undoing (perhaps reflecting the disoriented nature of his father's reasoning), Jack emphasizes the extent to which havoc in one's life breeds displacement, to which it can cause one to seek someone or something to blame, even if, as his father's displacements attest, the blame rests finally with oneself, or with nobody.

What is at stake for Jack in the unfolding of his father's tale, and of his father's friend's tale, is far from readily apparent. One of Jack's concerns is certainly his horror at having seen a corpse fished from the pond, the corpse of a man he knew. "It's not him," Jack says as the men pull the "dripping thing" into the boat. "It's something else that has been in there for years." Jack's denial of the horror in his recollection suggests that denial is still with him. Like that "something else" he imagines briefly, a vague substitute for the true object of horror, the ponderousness of this denial resides in him even now, having similarly been "in there for years." Beyond fishing up a youthful trauma, Jack's act of telling also attempts to come to grips with his father's dissolution — with the destabilizing of the authority figure of his childhood. "I don't think Dad really believed it," Jack says, reflecting on his father's comments about what "women can do to you," adding, "I think he just didn't know who to blame or what to say." Jack's "thinking" implies he is still searching for answers, that he is learning that the third thing is just one of many things that killed off his father, some of which he is only now beginning to fathom. Thus like his father, who displaces immediate concerns, blaming himself and women and fish and air attacks for defeats in his life, Jack likewise displaces not only a grisly spectacle of his boyhood but also lingering questions and concerns about his father, cushioning them in the protective layers of his narrative.[16]

Jack's central concern is buried deepest in these layers and is glimpsed only in the interstices of the story's weave, or — to make things easier — in an earlier version of the story. Inserted between what will eventually become the opening paragraphs of the later story, the second paragraph of "Dummy" originally read:

For me, Dummy's death signalled the end of my extraordinarily long childhood, sending me forth, ready or not, into the world of men — where defeat and death are more in the natural order of things.[17]

Because the literal references to Jack's transition in "The Third Thing" are unspoken, are in effect buried, his residual yearnings — because they are "left out," a la Hemingway — seem all the more powerful. Despite the increased hardness of the later story, the original emotional core remains, conveying in rather more subtle fashion Jack's hard-boiled nostalgia, his

or pull down our already-falling-down walls; even if freedom lies in the knowledge, as Carver's survivors tend to discover, that all our houses are borrowed, whether we own them or not.

In "Where I'm Calling From" we find another man trying to come to grips with alcoholism, this time within the enclosed environment of an alcohol treatment home. Unlike Meyers in his compartment, or Lloyd in his garrett, or Sandy's husband in his insular living room — men self-barricaded in ways as offensive to others as they are destructive to self — this speaker's confinement, like Wes's, is both positive and necessary. Until lately he has insulated himself with the buffering torpor booze provides, his addiction both a reaction to and the cause of his failing marriage; now he locks himself up voluntarily in "Frank Martin's drying out facility." Arriving at Frank Martin's dead drunk (but a stronger version of Wes in the end), he exchanges one state of insularity for another, taking refuge from his prior refuge, the one that was killing him. Sitting on the porch with another recovering drunk, J. P., he takes further comfort in the story his new friend has to tell.[9]

It is significant that throughout most of the story Carver leaves his characters sitting where they are. Protected yet still exposed to the chill of the outer world, the porch is a liminal space existing between the internal security of the cure-in-progress and the lure, and danger, of the outer world. On the porch, the narrator and J. P. are at once sheltered and vulnerable, their immediate physical surroundings an objective correlative to the transitional state of their minds and wills. Beyond the "green hill" they see from the porch, as Frank Martin tells them, is Jack London's house, the place where the famous author lived until "alcohol killed him." Beyond that — much farther north — is the "Yukon," the fictive *topos* of London's "To Build a Fire," a place where, as the narrator recalls later, a man will "actually . . . freeze to death if he can't get a fire going." With his wet clothes London's figure is hardly well-insulated, even though, ironically, he's bundled up in the manner of Carver's story's two strongest figures: J. P.'s wife, Roxy (whose "big knuckles" have broken her husband's nose) wears both a "coat" and "a heavy sweater"; Frank Martin, hard-edged and tough and looking like a "prizefighter," keeps his "sweater buttoned all the way up."

Sitting alone, enjoying the transitional comforts of the porch, Carver's speaker fails to recall, or subconsciously omits, the sad conclusion of London's tale — that, at the mercy of the elements, London's man eventually freezes, his life extinguished along with his fire. Still upset about Tiny's "seizure," it seems, he chooses not to think of the extreme consequences of ill-prepared exposure to the outer world, nor does he remind himself that death had entered the heart of the sanctuary only days before, this time without claiming its prize. Subject also to bodily complaints, J. P. suffers from the "shakes" and the narrator from an occasional "jerk in [his] shoulder"; like Tiny, the fat electrician from Santa Rosa, J. P. and his friend are each in their own way overpowered by biology, by nature. Their bodies adjust and compensate as they recover, as do their minds. And just as love was once "something that was out of [J. P.'s] hands" — a thing which set his "legs atremble" and filled him "with sensations that were carrying him every which way" — the aftermath of drinking is for the narrator superseded in intensity only by death, the ultimate spasm, a force proceeding from within as well as from without, over which insulation has no power at all.

Before "going inside," Frank recommends a bit of reading, namely *The Call of the Wild*; "We have it inside if you want to read something," he tells J. P. and the speaker. "It's about this animal that's half dog and half wolf." The narrator is similarly divided, torn by inner impulses. At the outset of his first visit, Frank had taken him aside, saying, "We can help you. If you want help and want to listen to what we say"; thinking now in retrospect, he admits, "I didn't know if they could help me or not. Part of me wanted help. But there was another part." Partly civilized, partly wild, he is in a very real way protecting himself from *himself*. His retreat at Frank Martin's is an attempt at self-domestication that, considering his present predicament, has failed him before. Caught up in a veritable war of selves, blown by the aftermath of addiction, literally vibrating in his chair, he is "not out of the woods yet," as he tells J. P. "In-between women," Skenazy writes, "in-between homes, in-between drinks, the narrator locates himself in his disintegration."[10] In this in-between world he begins to come to terms with disintegration, and begins imagining ways to reintegrate and rebuild.

Above all he wants "to listen," as Frank Martin says, though it is not Frank he chiefly listens to but J. P. "Keep talking, J. P.," he says early on.

"You better keep talking," he says, interjecting this and like phrases throughout the story in the manner of a refrain. Emergence from hardened insularity is connected to listening, to intensive listening. It is as necessary for him as *telling* is for J. P. and for Carlyle in "Fever," who emerges from a psychological and physical ordeal by unloading his pent-up turmoils verbally on his babysitter. In "Where I'm Calling From," the process of coming out involves *moving into* the narrative of another, entering imaginatively into a discourse which, arising of the communal act of storytelling, is at once familiar and unfamiliar. Since "commiseration instigates recuperation," as Arthur Saltzman observes of this tale, J. P.'s story initiates by means of both fellowship and displacement the continuation of the narrator's own story — and, if he is lucky, the reassembly of his fragmented life.[11] But there are perils as well as benefits in such transactions, in sharing stories. In "Will You Please Be Quiet, Please," a secure, relatively happy man becomes distraught at hearing the tale of his wife's infidelity, a tale she tells him herself. Rudy's recollection of his overweight classmates in "Fat," a misfired attempt at warm conversation, embitters his bitter wife all the more. In "Sacks," a son self-enclosed by concerns meets his father briefly in an airport, and hearing the story of his father's adultery, cuts himself off from his father for good, utterly alienated by the old man's confession.

Before *Cathedral*, extended verbal transaction — if transaction takes place at all — usually constitutes perilous intercourse indeed. In "Where I'm Calling From," however, as in other stories of this volume, Carver would have us believe otherwise. "I'm listening," the speaker says, waiting for J. P. to go on with his tale. "It's helping me to relax, for one thing. It's taking me away from my own situation." J. P.'s story helps him do more than merely "relax." Listening, and the imagination required for close listening, takes him away from his "own situation" even as it brings him closer to the heart of his problems. His inner crisis is externalized in J. P.'s story, both in the pairing of their present circumstances and in the details of his friend's narration — in such odd details, in fact, as the "well" J. P. fell into as a boy. Like the chimneys from which J. P. makes his livelihood later in life (narrow, tubular enclosures associated with the family to whom he becomes attached — they run a chimney-sweep business), the well is a trap, a darkly insulating prison; it represents the extent to which J. P. senses, enclosed until very recently in a bottle, he has hit "bottom" in the present trajectory of his life.[12] For the narrator and J. P. alike, the well represents the pitfalls of experience, the dark places they have found themselves in, places they are extricated from ultimately only through the intervening efforts of others. Like J. P. "hollering" at the bottom of the well, the narrator waits for a dropline of his own, his "line out" being (along with his willingness to reform) the telephone. By the end of the story he has tried calling his wife twice and is about to call his "girlfriend," hoping to reestablish contact with the women in his life, not to mention with the outer world — hence the story's title. Not by any means out of the woods yet, though, he still wavers in his resolve. In one of the story's last lines, thinking of his girlfriend, he says, "Maybe I'll call her first" — suggesting, given what we know about her drinking, that this line out may send him tumbling back into the hole. Torn between the warmth of stability and the chill of the outer world, between civilization and wilderness, he continues his war with himself.

Mildly obsessed with the women in his life, he has two layers of female protection, in a sense buffering him from the world. It is not surprising, then, that his life and J. P.'s story intersect finally in a woman's kiss. Rather more hopeful than the peacock in "Feathers" — one man's radiant token of bliss he'll never know — Roxy's kiss is a token of "luck" emphasizing more than this speaker's need for help from without, for a rope down the well of his life. As a gesture, Roxy's kiss underscores the degree to which women provide him much-needed security; he has in the past depended on women, perhaps, as much as he has on drink, or does now on the captivating flow of J. P.'s narrative. Our sense of this man's greatest personal security, in fact, comes with a recollection of his wife and him in the bedroom — that morning, long ago, when the landlord came around to paint the house:

I push the curtain away from the window. Outside, this old guy in white coveralls is standing next to his ladder. The sun is just starting to break over the mountains. The old guy and I look each other over. It's the landlord, all right — this old guy in coveralls. But his coveralls are too big for him. He needs a shave, too. And he's wearing this baseball cap to cover his bald head. Goddamn it, I think, if he isn't a weird old fellow. And a wave of happiness comes over me that I'm not him — that I'm me and that I'm inside this bedroom with my wife. (145)

Seated on "the front steps" in the chill air beyond the porch, the narrator warms himself with this memory of the past, a memory seemingly triggered by the kiss he gets from Roxy (before she and J. P. "go in," leaving him outside alone). He associates his past "happiness," then, with being "inside" with his wife in the bedroom, suggesting not only how much women are integral to his well-being but also how beneficial certain walls and enclosures have been to him at various times. "Outside," as in the form of a strange, skinny old man, are reminders of toil and old age, and, as before, of what lies beyond that — illness and decrepitude and death. "[I]nside," on the contrary, there is security and leisure, embodied by a laughing wife, the enveloping comforts of a warm bed, and the recognition of his circumstances as being as secure as they then were.

Thus the contact the narrator makes with an old man one morning is recapitulated by his contact with a younger man years later, though contact is closer now since both men are "outside," and working together to find ways back in. Epitomized in the gesture of Roxy's kiss, the intersecting of their lives and stories initiates a recuperation that may or may not get them, as J. P. says, "back on the track." With disruptions in time and in narrative continuity that mirror the psychic state of the narrator, the story wanders from man to man in its focus, intertwining the individual threads of their stories, rendering them oddly inseparable, fusing them in the brotherly knit of the text. By promoting such healthy complicity, such intersections, "Where I'm Calling From" embodies and dramatizes our tendency to discover ourselves in the stories of others, to complicate other lives with our own as we collaborate toward understanding, toward liberation from the confinements that kill.

"A Small, Good Thing" presents a similar intersecting of lives, more disparate, but with problems no less vivid and serious. It is the story of a couple dealing with the loss of a child, and of the consolation they find eventually, haphazardly, in the company of a baker; it is a story about grief and worry and fear, and about how disaster can crack one's insulating though eggshell-thin sense of habitual security. It is also, like "The Third Thing" and other stories, about how the narratives of others can cushion the violent unsettling such cracking brings on. As in "Where I'm Calling From," recovery is connected to listening, to opening oneself to others through channels of verbal interaction. In this story, however —

perhaps because its central figures, Ann and Howard Weiss, are simultaneously more stable and more emotionally vulnerable than J. P. and his friend, and because the story evokes a greater sense of affirmation in general — the liberating aspects of attentive listening are more noticeable. With a fullness and optimism unequalled in any other story, Carver dramatizes here what William Stull calls "talk that works."[13] He provides here an answer to the failures his characters have been subject to all along, failures of characters in all of his books, who talk and listen with characteristically poor results.[14]

Corresponding to this new fullness of possibility, the story itself swells to new proportions (revised from its original form as "The Bath"), reflecting aesthetically and spatially the kind of psychological and spiritual expansion taking place within, on the level of theme. As Kathleen Shute writes of the revised story, "Carver not only confronts death here — a victory in itself — but goes on to record the life after, the agony and resulting growth of those who survive."[15] Thus "what began in 'The Bath' as an existential chronicle of Hopelessville," Stull writes, "becomes in 'A Small, Good Thing' a rich demonstration of what George Eliot called 'the secret of deep human sympathy.' "[16]

"So far," we hear of Howard Weiss, "he had kept away from any real harm, from those forces he knew existed and that could cripple or bring down a man if the luck went bad, if things suddenly turned." As it is for J. P.'s friend, "luck" is of crucial importance to Howard; its capriciousness, he understands, dictates over the details of his world — has in fact allowed "forces" to insinuate themselves into the placid interior of his life, forces manifesting themselves, after the initial blow in the form of a car, in the ominous calls of the baker. Howard's insular bubble of security on the point of bursting, he remains sealed in his "car for a minute" in the driveway, his leg beginning to "tremble" as he considers the gravity of his circumstances. Trying to "deal with the present situation in a rational manner," his motor control is almost as erratic as that of Frank Martin's clients. Similarly affected, Ann's teeth begin to "chatter" as fear begins to take over, as she realizes that she and her husband are "into something now, something hard." Like recovering alcoholics, both are afflicted by an irrational power in the face of which rationality is useless. The walls of their once-secure and self-enclosed familial world have, thanks to a bit of bad luck, crumbled with alarming speed, such that Weiss's lives are literally shaken by circumstance.

As the focal figure of the story, Ann comes across as both more preoccupied and more sensitive than her husband, not necessarily because her parental (maternal) attachment to the boy is greater than Howard's, but because she is afforded more interior space throughout the story. Despite the intensity of her preoccupation in their days-long vigil, therefore, she momentarily glimpses new walls around her, walls self-erected in the tide of catastrophe. "For the first time," the narrator says, describing Ann's realization after many hours in the hospital, "she felt they were together in it, this trouble." Realizing she has shut herself off to everything but her son and his condition, she acknowledges "She hadn't let Howard into it, though he was there and needed all along. She felt glad to be his wife." If the disruptive force of calamity clarifies, it also causes both Ann and her husband, hemmed in now by fear and dread, to project outward as they seek respite from confinement. Worry insulating them as security had before, they stand staring "out at the parking lot." They don't "say anything. But they seem . . . to feel each other's insides now, as though the worry had made them transparent in a perfectly natural way." Their interior state of affairs is "natural," of course, because it is *nature*, and their powerlessness in the face of it, that makes them transparent, that prompts them, fire-distilled now by mutual concern, to gaze out the window in a way that recalls J. P. and his friend on the porch. "This spiritual transparency," Stull notes, "makes a stark contrast to the existential opacity of the original characters" in "The Bath."[17] The "ability of one character to empathize with another's inarticulation," Michael Gearhart writes of this story, "is a rarity in Carver's fiction" — and a phenomenon, we might add, unprecedented in Carver's work until this story.[18]

The verbal connections taking place in the story, are unprecedented as well. As in "Where I'm Calling From," the act of exchanging stories serves as a refuge, though here an even more compensatory one. Ann and Howard end up in a bakery, giving up the oppressive environment of the hospital and a house full of painful momentoes for a warmer, more spacious setting. The verbal transaction in the bakery is for both husband and wife (to use the doctor's mistaken diagnosis regarding Scotty's "deep sleep") a kind of "restorative measure"; at the hands of the baker the

Weisses are doctored as their son could not be. Unlike J. P. and his friend, however, they are consoled by a man who cannot truly identify or empathize, a man as ironically unlike them as anybody could be. "I don't have any children myself," the baker tells Howard and Ann, "so I can only imagine what you must be feeling." Still, sparked by his power to "imagine" their grief, he begins his tale of "loneliness, and of . . . what it was like to be childless all these years," offering them if nothing else at least the consolation of knowing that they know what they are going to miss. Thus husband and wife listen, and listening, enter the baker's world — his story — to temporarily escape their own. "They listened carefully," the narrator says, drawing special attention to the act through repetition: "they listened to what the baker had to say."

Elsewhere in *Cathedral*, hearing and listening are treated in less optimistic terms. In "Careful," Lloyd's metaphorical deafness to the world is figured in the literal blockage of his ear with wax. In "Vitamins," a similar if more general deafness finds its emblem in the form of a dismembered, dried-out human ear. But in other stories — in "Fever" and "Where I'm Calling From," for instance — characters indeed turn their ears to others, and come away better for it. "I got ears," blind Robert says in "Cathedral," affirming, in spite of his handicap, that "Learning never ends." "Intimacy," one of Carver's last stories, features a fiction writing narrator who calls himself "all ears," at once a plunderer of experience (like his predecessor in "Put Yourself in My Shoes") and a meticulous listener, a person who by way of listening carefully reconstructs memory to reorder the disorder of his past. In "A Small, Good Thing," more strikingly than ever, telling and listening are beneficial, recuperative activities. What is crucial here is not so much the substance of the stories characters tell as the process of telling. ("I was interested," J. P.'s friend says of J. P.'s tale; "But I would have listened if he'd been going on about how one day he'd decided to start pitching horseshoes.") Enveloped in the baker's tale, Ann and Howard listen and listen, escaping the still unthinkable reality of their present circumstances by entering the stifling, insulated, private life of their host, thus beginning their slow journey out of the darkness of grief. Though it is still dark outside, it is "like daylight" inside the bakery. Warmed by the light and the ovens and the sweet rolls they eat, revived by mutual compassion, Ann and Howard do "not think of leaving."

From the shadowy, overdetermined world of "The Bath," then, where the tiny enclosure of a bathtub provides a sole comfort for characters ("Fear made him want to take a bath," the original narrator says of Howard), we traverse to the indoor daylight of the bakery, where food and talk and commiseration actually do make a difference, if not redeeming characters of their misery at least affording them comfort, allowing them to see that loneliness and hardship and death are part of the natural order of things and that as people they can share their aloneness. The welcome light of possibility and potential self-regeneration is also reflected in the overall shape of the story; "A Small, Good Thing" is two-thirds again as long as the original story and the longest story Carver ever published. "I went back to that one," he said in an interview,

as well as several others, because I felt there was unfinished business that needed attending to. The story hadn't been told originally; it had been messed around with, condensed and compressed in "The Bath" to highlight the qualities of menace that I wanted to emphasize . . . so in the midst of writing these other stories for Cathedral I went back to "The Bath" and tried to see what aspects of it needed to be enhanced, redrawn, reimagined.[19]

Enhanced and redrawn, the story is nevertheless still in many ways characteristic of Carver. The "one in a million circumstance" of Scotty's "hidden occlusion," as Kathleen Shute observes, demonstrates that "even in this more optimistic universe, a blind and inexplicable randomness still lurks, shaping and destroying at will."[20] Thus "even as [Carver] makes the characters more sympathetic," Stull notes, "he remains true to the harsh existential premises of the story."[21] Carver remains true to himself, in other words, altering his artistic methods but preserving the core of his vision as he moves from contraction to expansion. Comparing its spareness to the fullness of Cathedral, Carver says of What We Talk About When We Talk About Love, "Everything I thought I could live without I just got rid of, I cut out . . . It felt like I'd gone as far in that direction as I wished to go."[22] Radically changing direction, reexploring old subjects while delving into unfinished business, Carver illustrates in this writerly expansion how fully an artist can break down the self-fashioned walls of style and still maintain his signature. Not unlike a few of his more fortunate characters, Carver exhanges an enclosing environment for greater capaciousness, for a new but not unfamiliar direction, and, we tend to suppose, for a new sense of himself.

More frequently anthologized than any other story by Carver, "Cathedral" charts the coming out of a self-insulated figure more dramatically than ever before, a man who, unlike Myers running from the world on a train bound for nowhere, begins to sense the seriousness of his insularity. Hemmed in by insecurity and prejudice, buffered by drink and pot and by the sad fact, as his wife says, that he has no "friends," he is badly out of touch with his world, his wife, and himself. But as in "A Small, Good Thing" and "Where I'm Calling From," and less optimistically in "Chef's House," he emerges from enclosure and transcends his self-strictures, although this story affords neither release nor any semi-conscious decision, but rather a nonverbal act — an odd, unspoken transaction taking place between him and his blind guest. As is often the case with Carver's characters, talk fails here, and yet this man's failure is more than made up for by the connection he succeeds in making at last, by the self-liberating results of his trial.

Recalling Howard and Ann Weiss, and Wes in his idyllic retreat, his narrow, sheltered world is abruptly threatened from without. The appearance of his wife's friend Robert constitutes, at least at the outset, an invasion of his hermetic existence. "A blind man in my house was not something I looked forward to," he says, and later adds, "Now this same blind man was coming to sleep in my house." His territorial impulses, spurred by insecurity and repulsion and fear, make for what Skenazy calls an "evening of polite antagonism between the two men."[23] His buried hostility, we are led to suppose, is rooted in part in Robert's association with his wife's past, a past that intimidates him — particularly her former marriage, a subject with which he is obsessed. Simultaneously fascinated by and reluctant to hear the blind man's story ("my wife filled me in with more details than I cared to know," he says; "I made a drink and sat at the kitchen table to listen") he at least indirectly seeks, in his wife's dealings with Robert, some sense of himself, of self-image. Like J. P.'s friend, this man's identity is connected to his bond with a female, a bond he needs to see perpetually reinforced — although, justly perturbed by his insensitivity, his wife does not give him the reinforcement he craves. Referring to his wife's conversation with Robert in the living room, he says, "I waited in vain to hear my name on my wife's sweet lips." His muddled search for self involves a continual gauging and protecting of the autocratic status of his name. A year earlier, hearing a taped conversation between his wife and her friend, he'd been startled to hear his "own name in the mouth of [a] stranger, this blind man." Determined to assert himself, ineffective as his methods may seem, he blankets his wife's past the way he has lately blanketed his present — with insulating self-absorbency. Summing up his wife's prior life, he calls her ex-husband her "officer," adding, "Why should he have a name?" No ideal listener, and short on compassion, he predicates the names and stories of others under the heading of his own tyrannical if precarious identity, listening for purposes of self-validation, relegating the rest of experience, including Robert's marriage, to a place "beyond [his] understanding."

It is fitting that Robert, the invader in the house, is insulated only physically, left in the dark only by his handicap. Extremely outgoing and friendly, he has done "a little of everything," from running a sales distributorship to traveling in Mexico to broadcasting "ham radio." His activities, unlike those of his host, take him out into the world, his booming voice having extended as far as "Alaska" and "Tahiti" on the airwaves before making its way into the narrator's home. Unlike the baker and J. P. — restrained men in comparison — Robert is pure blazing personality, an extradurable and appropriate guide, a man capable of pulling his host from his shell. (Like the Weisses, however, Robert also is grieving, having just lost his wife; "I know about skeletons," he says, regarding the show on TV). As Robert's host fails to describe what he sees on the television, Robert listens, and having "listened" to failure, takes charge of the situation. "Hey, listen to me," he says, activated suddenly by his host's admission of verbal defeat. "Will you do me a favor? I got an idea. Why don't you find us some heavy paper. And a pen. We'll do something. We'll draw one together. Get us a pen and some heavy paper. Go on, bub, get the stuff." Robert's initiative here, and the remedy he momentarily employs, suggests that verbal handicaps — not to mention the larger problems of which they are symptoms — are like unto blindness, debilitations stemming from the willed blindness of oversight, of poor insight, of ignorance. The way Robert takes charge and plays the role of the teacher (his gray beard implying, on some quiet level, wisdom) suggests that handicaps are first and foremost challenges, hurdles we surmount and pass over.

Regarding the joint project of the drawing, Michael Vander Weele writes, "most of the communication in this story comes through shared non-verbal work, as expression that stops short of the effort and commonality of speech."[24] A true case of the blind leading the blind, drawing the cathedral is a "gesture of fraternity," as Howe observes, which, like the meal preceding it, promotes human contact and finally nudges the narrator, if only temporarily, out of his self-contained world.[25] The subject and product of their mutual efforts, the cathedral — like all of Carver's symbols — represents mainly itself, an old thing made of stone, though its metaphorical resonances (concerning common humanity, benevolence and good will, patient human effort and fortitude in the act of "a-spiring") are palpable, if typically non-insistent, in the story.[26] Curiously, the speaker ultimately ends up within the walls of his own handmade cathedral. "I was in my house," he says when he finishes, eyes still tightly closed, bringing to mind the "box" he drew when he and Robert began, a figure that "could have been the house [he] lived in." What begins, therefore, as the enclosing spatial configuration of his home — and of his present level of awareness, we guess — gradually swells in proportion to become something more spacious, something awesome and utterly new, its interior depths as enlightening to him as bakeries and bedrooms are comforting to others.

"As in D. H. Lawrence's story 'The Blind Man,' " Goodheart observes, "blindness becomes a metaphor for imagination: the power of the mind to ascend to the spires."[27] "I didn't feel like I was inside anything," the narrator says, still unwilling to open his eyes, in a sense blinding himself in order to see. While Myers "close[s] his eyes" to whatever encroaches on his personal life (his voluntary blindness as bad as Lloyd's deafness), this man finds not escape or evasion but finally discovery in self-enclosure, a discovery made possible by his willingness to delve into that inner vestibule of self, where selfishness gives way at last to self-awareness. A man obsessed with the faculty of vision ("Imagine," he says of Robert's wife early on, "a woman who could never see herself as she was seen in the eyes of her loved one"), he clings now to a miraculous glimpse of a world beyond insular life, remaining willingly blind to the distracting re-

ality of his former world, even as Robert calls him back. "It was like
nothing else in my life up to now," he says, staggered by new awareness,
adding, in the story's final sentence, "It's really something." The indefiniteness of his language — he is usually more glib than he seems here —
expresses both the sheer incomprehensibility of his revelation and the
fact that he registers it as such. He falls into "depths of feeling that he
need not name to justify," as one critic writes, feelings of an intensity un-
matched anywhere else in Carver's fiction.[28]

Transcendence, of course, has lurked in Carver's work since the earliest stories, evidenced by the "impossible changes" Ralph Wyman under-
goes in "Will You Please Be Quiet, Please?" where jealousy and self-pre-
occupation are neutralized in the end by human contact, by something
much larger than words. Just as Ann Weiss wants "her words to be her
own" after the death of her son, shopping for a private vocabulary of
grief, the man in "Cathedral" gropes for words weighty enough to fit his
experience, and failing gloriously in that, settles for indefinites. Impossi-
bly changed, reduced to semi-inarticulateness, he keeps his eyes fastened
shut, wavering between awareness and habitual existence, there in his
new and newly spacious enclosure. He is "no longer inside himself," as
Skenazy writes, "if not quite outside, no longer alone, if not quite intimate."[29]

The tonal shift in the final sequence of the story, then, marked by the
mild ethereality flooding the last lines, itself illustrates the opening up the
narrator has undergone, and is yet to undergo. Like Robert, on a journey
by train, dropping in on friends and relatives, trying to get over the loss
of his wife, the narrator is also on a journey, one signaled by signposts in
his language and played out by the events of the story he tells. (Early in
the story, he feels momentarily "sorry for the blind man," his insulated
hardness beginning to soften; as the walls of his resentment noticeably
crack, he watches with "admiration" as Robert eats, recognizing that
Robert's handicap is no impairment to his performance at the dinner
table.) This man's destination, like that of all Carver's travelers — whether
they leave home or not — is necessarily a confining one. But it is also a
destination where one's sense of shared confinement makes for hereto-
fore unknown freedoms. "What's a cathedral without people?" Robert
asks, bidding his host to add a touch of humanity to the drawing, to "put

Consciously or otherwise, he draws out the likeness between his father and himself, likening the way his father once supported him (on "his shoulders") to the way he is himself financially supporting his own as well as his father's family now. Like the "elephant" he imagines his father to be, extra strong, extra benevolent, he plods along now bearing his family, and with elephantine patience has not let them fall. "I put more checks in the mail," he says, concluding his first tally of obligations. "Then I held my breath and waited." His mention of "the swing" in his dream further echoes his daughter's comments about his grandchildren, who had drawn "pictures of the swing sets" at the motel he'd stayed in when he visited, and reinforces his sense of obligation; though they ask nothing of him, his grandchildren depend on him, too.

Standing beside the highway on his way to work, he enacts a gesture he remembers from the dream, raising his arms and holding them out "for balance" as he had on his father's shoulders. Unlike the embraces in "Boxes," or the sign language in "Menudo," this gesture is uniquely personal, a gesture aimed at equanimity, at psychic equilibrium on the part of the dreamer. "[S]tanding there like that, like a goof" on the roadside, he hopes to "balance" the past with the present; to offset old memories of drunkenness with his more recent sobriety, to mitigate residual guilt by weighing it against those compensatory tokens of restoration he has lately, ungrudgingly, bestowed. In another sense, he seeks to balance his meager successes with the individual failures of his kin, and balance his resistance to circumstances in general with, as the story's ending suggests, unconditional acceptance.

Like the historian in "Blackbird Pie," this man reassesses his predicament, examining his motives in a kind of "self-reading" now familiar to us, knowing as we do the figures and situations of the last stories. "[A]ll of a sudden," he says, "I could imagine how it must have sounded to my family when I'd threatened them with a move to Australia . . . Now, thinking about their laughter, I had to laugh, too. *Ha, ha, ha.* That was exactly the sound I made there at the table— *ha, ha, ha* — as if I'd read somewhere how to laugh." In a curious way an audience unto himself, auditing not only his personal motivations but the very sound of his voice, he begins to see his world — not unlike the man in "Cathedral" — from a different perspective. Engaging in reflective self-dissociation, he

realizes that unlike birds who move "from one part of the valley to another," he can't (or doesn't actually want to) fly off to escape the crush of
obligation. He understands, finally, that "Australia" is an empty threat,
pure self-deception, understanding in a way that Donna in "Vitamins"
cannot, her heart desperately set on the illusory glimmer of "Portland,"
and as Leo in "What Is It?" cannot, banking his few remaining hopes on
an equally illusory day of the week. "[O]nce I understood this," the man
in "Elephant" says, sitting in his kitchen over morning coffee, "once I understood I wouldn't be going there — or anywhere else, for that matter — I began to feel better." As George notes slightly later, his friend is
indeed "in training"; he is a blue-collar existential athlete of sorts, a late
twentieth century Sisyphus learning the hard way that toil and daily obligation is only as bad as you make it, contingent on perspective and the
set of one's mind. Wishing the best for each member of his family — taking a final inventory as he walks — he says he feels he has "the right to
whistle if [he] wanted to," implying that there are always degrees of freedom within constraint, and that there is usually "lots to hope for."

    "'Hey, get in, buddy,'" George says, pulling up in his car — cutting
short, one tends to think, the narrator's newfound freedom, the release
accompanying that sudden, wholesale acceptance of his "load." George's
intrusion seems to disrupt the serenity of the narrator's mood, and his
address smacks of abduction, but his presence allows for yet another release in the form of the car — an extension, in fact, of the narrator's
newfound freedom.[20] "I borrowed some money and had this baby over-
hauled," George explains while accelerating (toying with his unlit cigar,
he is the proud father of a "baby" that costs him dearly — he's had to
borrow to support it). George has discovered, as his coworker has, that
not only do responsibilities and obligations sometimes fail to drag one
down, they even afford uncanny liberty. Identifying closely with
George — they share an identical laugh ("ha, ha, ha") — the narrator di-
rects his final question as much to himself as to his friend: "What are you
waiting for, George?" he asks, encouraging George to step on the gas. He
has begun to learn at last just how futile "waiting" and holding one's
breath can be, and how unnecessary. Although they face the company
time clock soon, he and George streak "down that road in [George's] big
unpaid-for car," proving that even the smallest freedoms can be exhilarat-

ing, and that borrowed freedom is freedom nevertheless — is for some of us, for all of Carver's characters, the only real freedom we know.

In "Whoever Was Using This Bed" Carver falls back on a few familiar devices — the wrong number caller, insomnia — and in the process reinvigorates them, perhaps because the "obsession" to which he links them is new: the subject of human mortality. Death has been present in Carver's work from the beginning, of course, but only obliquely — only, as Tobias Wolff observes, as "an atmosphere of malign possibility." But in "his last stories and poems," Wolff writes, Carver "dragged the beast out of the corner and stared it in the face."[21] While the poems deal much more specifically, and autobiographically, with the "beast" ("What the Doctor Said" comes to mind, the title saying it all), "Whoever" provides a humorous, comprehensive look at human powerlessness in the face of oblivion, as well as at our strategies for compensating for such debility. [22]

"The call comes in the middle of the night," says Jack, the story's narrator, "and it nearly scares us to death." Jack and his wife Iris are flung into wakefulness by a wrong number caller, and, momentarily terrified, are prompted to conversation. Too jumpy to go back to sleep, they talk away the rest of the night, their conversation occupying most of the story. Focusing at first on the subject of sickness, their conversation moves eventually to terminal illness and dying, yet their dialogue is so unfocused that a good amount of talking goes on while not a whole lot gets said. At one point, when Iris grows fearful at the idea of living like a "vegetable," Jack tries to comfort her, saying,

"It won't happen to us. It won't," I say. "Don't worry about any of it, okay? We're fine, Iris, and we're going to stay fine. In any case, that time's a long time off. Hey, I love you. We love each other, don't we? That's the important thing. That's what counts. Don't worry, honey." (327)

Endeavoring to calm his wife, Jack's deeper concerns — concerns as grave as Iris's — are given away by his language. The repetition of words ("won't," "worry," "fine," "love"), not to mention the urgency of his tone, betray that he is trying to convince himself as much as her of their safety. Considering the rhetorical economy of the story — one of Carver's fullest, for sure, and the most dialogue-packed — it is hard not to see talking itself as a reaction to menace, to the threat of personal suffering and death. In a similar sense, "What We Talk About When We Talk About Love" presents a symposium on a subject so elusive and powerful that its discoursers can only talk around it, and are left literally in the dark in the end. Jack and Iris, however, deal with a much darker subject, a subject even more awesome and slippery, talking and talking in an attempt as much to ward it off as to understand it fully.

Exhausted and edgy the following day, Jack says, "I feel as if I've come to a place I never thought I'd have come to . . . It's a strange place. It's a place where a little harmless dreaming and then some sleepy, early-morning talk has led me into considerations of death and annihilation." The "place" Jack speaks of, that vertiginous realm of existential reflection, is one he both enters with words and, with varying degrees of anxiety, covers over with words, trying to bury it again as best he can. It is a place both familiar and starkly alien, a place he finds himself in suddenly, signaled by a phone call, itself a form of verbal transmission. The caller's desperation, infecting Jack and Iris in turn, is grounded in a desire identical to theirs: the desire to be saturated with language. "Bud," she pleads, unable to believe that Jack is Jack and not Bud, "talk to me, please."

"She's more on my side than her own side," Jack says of his wife, surveying the bed as he returns from the phone — a statement echoing in the halls of Carver's canon, from Nan's despairing glimpse of her husband's "arm flung out across her side of the bed" in "The Student's Wife," to the transplanted bedroom set in "Why Don't You Dance?," featuring "his side" and "her side," to Hughes's unhappy observation of his wife "scrunched on to about ten inches of mattress," sleeping "on her side of the bed."[23] Such echoes reemphasize the power politics of the bedroom, the division drawn out in lines of romantic scrimmage. Like Nan, Jack is not so much troubled by distance and separation as he is by proximity. The sheer physicality of his wife's presence on his side of the bed is symptomatic of larger problems involving psychic space, problems having to do with what is ultimately the greatest freedom one can imagine: freedom of choosing life over death. The question of whether to give one's spouse authority to "pull the plug" evokes, as one reviewer says of Jack and Iris, "the extreme of intimacy their marriage implies."[24] Similarly in "Proposal," a late poem about Ray and Tess's marriage (which took place just months before Carver's death), the speaker exclaims, "Oh lovely, oh lethal entanglements," musing on a film romance in which Betty Davis kills her ex-lover. In another poem, "Wake Up" (also from *Waterfall*), a couple plays morbid games in the dungeon of Zurich's Kyborg Castle, the speaker placing his "head on the block" while his mate simulates the blow of decapitation with her hand.[25]

This is this kind of authority that Jack, who speaks earlier of a time he and his wife were "fistfighting" in their sleep, resists. "Don't unplug me," he says, having mulled too long over the question of the life-support machines. "Leave me hooked up just as long as possible," he insists. "Right to the bitter end."[26] Not unlike others in Carver country, Jack clings to what little control he has in death's kingdom, the realm of the uncontrollable. Like Hughes, rake in hand, facing the "big things" in his life by focusing on small things first, Jack needs the order of a well-made bed to offset the vast disorder of sleep's second self, a thing terrifyingly beyond the scope of personal jurisdiction. For him, the "strange place" they arrive at in their conversation precludes a return to preexistentialist innocence — it is like reading Sartre and then trying to forget about him. "I know I won't ever look at this bed again," Jack says, noticing the disarray of sheets and blankets around him, "without remembering it like this."

Try as he might, then, Jack is not the master of his world he would like to think he is. The story closes with one last phone call, and with Jack reproaching the caller for rudeness; but as he scolds he finds the words suddenly taken out of his mouth: his wife unplugs the phone. "[W]hile I'm trying to tell all this to the woman," he says, "while I'm trying to make myself understood, my wife moves quickly and bends over, and that's it. The line goes dead, and I can't hear anything." Once again, Jack tries to "tell all" in an effort to fill up the unknown, trying to cover over oblivion with words, and now, emblematically speaking, his worst fears suddenly come true. With the rhetorical finality of "that's it," accompanied by the adroitly placed cliche "dead" and the reverberating silence evoked by the final clause, Jack's powerlessness could not be more gravely emphasized. With no choice left in the matter, Jack's "extreme of intimacy" is embodied by his noticeable lack of autonomy. In "Blackbird Pie" being single spells out a frightening loss of identity, but in this story things are just the opposite — overintimacy in marriage makes for the dissolution of personal integrity, and a tendency toward lapsing into nonidentity.

"It looks like whoever was using this bed left in a hurry," Jack observes, underlining not only his obsessiveness about a tidy bed but also, evoked by the indefiniteness of the word "whoever," the kind of anonymity he senses arising of confrontations with the incomprehensible, with forces larger and more powerful than he can begin to imagine. "We could have been anybody," Hughes says on a similar note, describing his meeting with Amanda in the coffee shop, caught up in the pervasiveness and randomness of love's victimizations. Reducing himself and his wife alike to the indefinite "whoever," Jack suggests how little control we all have in everything, and how, talk as much as we like, we come and go in a hurry.

Carver's last story, "Errand," treats the subject of mortality much more directly, dealing with it in terms of his own life and its connection to art. In this story Carver aligns himself, and his image of himself as an artist, with Chekov, who died similarly of a lung condition. (Although Carver wrote the story, as he intimates at one point, months before he knew the severity of his illness, it nevertheless stands — unconscious or not — as an exploration of, if not a preparation for, his own premature death.)[27] To longtime devotees of Carver it is hardly a surprise to find Chekov serving as guide. Chekov was a primary mentor for Carver, a figure who had from the very beginning led Carver through ordeals and crises — emotional as well as artistic. More than twenty years before, Carver had published "Winter Insomnia," a poem in which he writes, "The mind is sick tonight/ It wishes Chekov were here to minister/ Something — three drops of valerian, a glass/ Of rose water/ anything, it wouldn't matter."[28] Chekov was as much a spiritual doctor for Carver as a literary model, a wellspring of insights intrinsic to his own life and work. ("And then suddenly," reads the Chekov exerpt Carver kept pinned above his desk, "everything became clear to him.")[29] Introducing A New Path To The Waterfall, Tess Gallagher describes Chekov's stories — and their partial incorporation into the volume — as "integral to [her and Ray's] spiritual survival," observing how the stories helped in completing not only a book but a life.[30]

"Errand," then, is not so much a departure from as the continuation of a trend. However, the style of the story constitutes a monumental departure from the norm, categorizable more along the lines of *Dostoevsky* (a screenplay, a bittersweet tribute to the master, cowritten by Gallagher and Carver) than within the normal context of his canon. "Errand" is in part a semi-historical documentary of Chekov's last years. It records the progression of his illness, along with a meticulous account of the hours preceding and succeeding the moment of his death.[31] Most striking, perhaps, is the conspicuous transformation of documentary into fiction in the story's final pages: what begins as a baldly historical account of incidents and dates culminates in a dreamy, hyper-detailed description of a fictional exchange between Chekov's widow and a bellhop.

Just as Chekov, as Carver writes in the story, "continually tried to minimalize the seriousness of his condition," behaving as though he might "throw off the disease"; and just as, despite the worsening of his symptoms, he "didn't stop" writing, so Carver kept the development of his illness a secret and, as Gallagher writes, "kept working, planning, believing in the importance of the time he had left . . . believing that he might, through some loop in fate, even get out." In this sense "Errand" is Carver's way of "practicing" for death (as Gallagher describes the decapitation games in "Wake Up"), of going through the motions, of letting imagination precede physical reality, so that his last hours in the world might come to seem as full of grace and control he envisioned those of his mentor to be.[32] Most importantly, by aligning himself with the Russian writer, Carver displaces his own impending death, exploring its implications in a way that, recalling Jack and Iris's interminable chitchat, confronts reality in the act of displacing it — and then takes displacement one step further by focusing on characters peripheral to the story's subject. If at first glance "Errand" seems as dissimilar to earlier stories in subject as in style, a close look reveals that Carver is still operating as he always has. Reflecting here more than ever the concerns of their creator, characters struggle for control in circumstances where individual control has been shaken, particularly toward the end of the story. With death now an adversary, these figures struggle harder than ever, their compensatory strategies, their footholds against the unknown, as distinctive as they are familiar to readers of Carver.

Ceremony is the main foothold, evidenced in the drinking of champagne, in Olga's vigil, and in her rigorous instructions to the bellhop re-

Ann Mason and 'Preservation' by Raymond Carver." *Modern Fiction Studies* 35.4 (Winter 1989): 689–98.

Herzinger, Kim A. "Introduction: On the New Fiction." *Mississippi Review* 40/41 (Winter 1985): 7–22.

Houston, Robert. "A Stunning Inarticulateness." *Nation* 233.1 (July 4, 1981): 23–25.

Howe, Irving. "Stories of Our Loneliness." *New York Times Book Review*, September 11, 1983.

Iser, Wolfgang. *The Implied Reader: Patterns of Communication in Prose Fiction from Bunyan to Beckett.* Baltimore: Johns Hopkins University Press, 1974.

Jakobson, Roman, and M. Halle. *Fundamentals of Language.* The Hague: Mouton, 1956.

Jenks, Tom. "Together in Carver Country." *Vanity Fair* 49.10 (October 1986): 114ff.

Karlsson, Ann-Marie. "The Hyperrealistic Short Story: A Postmodern Twilight Zone." *Criticism in the Twilight Zone: Postmodern Perspectives on Literature and Politics.* Eds. Danuta Zadworna-Fjellestad and Lennart Björk. Stockholm Studies in English 77. Stockholm: Almqvist, 1990. 144–53.

Kaufmann, David. "Yuppie Postmodernism." *Arizona Quarterly* 47.2 (Summer 1991): 93–116.

Kellerman, Stewart. "Grace Has Come into My Life." *New York Times Book Review*, May 15, 1988: 40.

Kermode, Frank. *The Sense of an Ending: Studies in the Theory of Fiction.* New York: Oxford University Press, 1968.

Kittredge, William. *We Are Not In This Together.* Port Townsend, WA: Graywolf Press, 1984.

——. "from *Hole in the Sky*." *Ploughshares* 16.4 (Winter 1990–91): 224–54.

Klinkowitz, Jerome. *Literary Disruptions: The Making of a Post-Contemporary American Fiction.* Urbana: University of Illinois Press, 1975.

——. "The Effacement of Contemporary American Literature." *College English* 42.4 (1980): 382–89.

Kubal, David. "Fiction Chronicle." *Hudson Review* 34.3 (Autumn 1981): 456–66.

Kuzma, Greg. "*Ultramarine*: Poems That Almost Stop the Heart." *Michigan Quarterly Review* 27.2 (Spring 1988): 355–63.

Lacan, Jacques. *The Language of the Self.* Trans. and ed. Anthony Wilden. New York: Delta, 1975.

Laing, R.D. *The Divided Self*. Baltimore: Penguin, 1965.

LeClair, Thomas. "Fiction Chronicle — June 1981." *Contemporary Literature* 23.1 (Winter 1982): 83–91.

Lentricchia, Frank. *After the New Criticism*. Chicago: University of Chicago Press, 1980.

Lepape, Pierre. "Carver et Vautrin: une même compassion." *Le Monde* 2100 (January 26, 1989): 12.

Lohafer, Susan. *Coming to Terms with the Short Story*. Baton Rouge: Louisiana State University Press, 1983.

Longinus. *Critical Theory Since Plato*. Ed. Hazard Adams. New York: Harcourt Brace, 1971. 77–102.

Lonnquist, Barbara C. "Narrative Displacement and Literary Faith: Raymond Carver's Inheritance from Flannery O'Connor." *Since Flannery O'Connor: Essays on the Contemporary American Short Story*. Eds. Loren Logsdon and Charles W. Mayer. An *Essays in Literature* Book. Macomb: Western Illinois University Press, 1987. 142–50.

Malamet, Elliott. "Raymond Carver and the Fear of Narration." *Journal of the Short Story in English* 17 (Autumn 1991): 59–74.

Mars-Jones, Adam. "Words for the Walking Wounded." *Times Literary Supplement* 4112 (January 22, 1982): 76.

McCaffery, Larry, ed. *Postmodern Fiction: A Bio-Bibliographical Guide*. Movements in the Arts Series 2. Westport: Greenwood, 1986.

McConnell, Frank D. *Four Postwar American Novelists*. Chicago: University of Chicago Press, 1977.

McInerney, Jay. "Raymond Carver: A Still, Small Voice." *New York Times Book Review* August 6, 1989.

McLuhan, Marshall. *The Gutenberg Galaxy: The Making of Typographic Man*. New York: Signet, 1969.

Meyer, Adam. "Now You See Him, Now You Don't, Now You Do Again: The Evolution of Raymond Carver's Minimalism." *Critique* 30.4 (Summer 1989): 239–51. Rpt. in Campbell, *Raymond Carver*, 143–58.

Miller, J. Hillis. "Poets of Reality." *The Secret Agent: A Casebook*. Ed. Ian Watt. London: Macmillan, 1973.

Mitchell, W.J.T., ed. *On Narrative*. Chicago: University of Chicago Press, 1981.

Nesset, Kirk. " 'This Word Love': Sexual Politics and Silence in Early Raymond Carver." *American Literature* 63.2 (June 1991): 293–313.

———. "The Final Stitch: Raymond Carver and Metaphor." Profils Americains 4 (Spring 1993): 21–27.

Newlove, Donald. "What We Talk About When We Talk About Love." Saturday Review April 1981: 77.

Olderman, Raymond M. Beyond the Waste Land: A Study of the American Novel in the Nineteen-Sixties. New Haven: Yale University Press, 1972.

Phillips, Jayne Anne. "The Secret Places of the Heart." New York 14.16 (April 20, 1981): 77–78.

Plath, James. "When Push Comes to Pull: Raymond Carver and the 'Popular Mechanics' of Divorce." Notes on Contemporary Literature 20.3 (May 1990): 2–4.

Pope, Dan. "The Post-Minimalist American Short Story or What Comes After Carver?" The Gettysburg Review 1.2 (Spring 1988): 331–42.

Richard, Claude. "La quotidienneté américaine." Trans. William Stull. Quinzaine Litteraire 439 (May 1–15, 1985): 8–9.

Richards, I. A. Practical Criticism. New York: Harcourt, Brace, and World, 1929.

Robinson, Marilynne. "Marriage and Other Astonishing Bonds." New York Times Book Review, May 15, 1988.

Robison, James C. "1969–1980: Experiment and Tradition." The American Short Story 1945–1980: A Critical History. Ed. Gordon Weaver. Boston: Twayne, 1983.

Saltzman, Arthur M. Understanding Raymond Carver. Columbia: University of South Carolina Press, 1988.

Sanders, Scott Russell. "Speaking a Word for Nature." Michigan Quarterly Review 26.4 (Fall 1987): 648–62. Rpt. in Delbanco, Writers and Their Craft, 394–407.

Scholes, Robert. The Fabulators. New York: Oxford University Press, 1967.

Seabrook, John. Interview with Richard Ford. "Of Bird Dogs and Tall Tales." Interview XIX.5 (May 1985): 128ff.

Shute, Kathleen Westfall. "Finding the Words: The Struggle for Salvation in the Fiction of Raymond Carver." Hollins Critic 24.5 (December 1987): 1–9. Rpt. in Campbell, Raymond Carver, 119–30.

Skenazy, Paul. "Peering through the Keyhole at Gloom." Los Angeles Times Book Review, June 26, 1988.

———. "Life in Limbo: Raymond Carver's Fiction." Enclitic 11.1 (21) (Fall 1988): 77–83.

Smith, Allan Lloyd. "Brain Damage: The Word and the World in Postmodernist

Writing." *Contemporary American Fiction*. Eds. Malcolm Bradbury and Sigmund
 Ro. Stratford-upon-Avon Studies, 2nd series. London: Edward Arnold, 1987.
 39–50.

Smitten, Jeffrey, and Ann Daghistany, eds. *Spatial Form in Narrative*. Ithaca: Cornell
 University Press, 1981.

Solotaroff, Ted. "Raymond Carver: Going Through the Pain." *American Poetry
 Review* 18.2 (March-April 1989): 47–49.

Stafford, William. "Suddenly Everything Became Clear to Him." *Washington* 5.3
 (November 1988): 103–06.

Stone, Robert. Untitled introductory statement to Carver, "Intimacy," *Esquire*
 (August 1986), 58.

Stull, William L. "Visions and Revisions." *Chariton Review* 10.1 (Spring 1984):
 80–86.

——. "Raymond Carver." *Dictionary of Literary Biography Yearbook* 1984. Ed. Jean
 W. Ross. Detroit: Gale, 1985. 233–45.

——. "Beyond Hopelessville: Another Side of Raymond Carver." *Philological
 Quarterly* 64.1 (Winter 1985): 1–15.

——. "Raymond Carver: A Bibliographical Checklist." *American Book Collector* ns
 8.1 (January 1987): 17–30.

——. "Raymond Carver Remembered: Three Early Stories." *Studies in Short
 Fiction*, 25.4 (Fall 1988): 461–77.

——. "Raymond Carver." *Dictionary of Literary Biography Yearbook* 1988. Ed. J.M.
 Brook. Detroit: Gale, 1989. 199–213.

——. "Raymond Carver." *Encyclopedia of World Literature in the 20th Century*. Eds.
 Steven R. Serafin and Walter D. Glanze. 4 vols. New York: Continuum, 1993.
 120–21. Supplement.

——, with Maureen P. Carroll. *Remembering Ray*. Santa Barbara: Capra, 1993.

Tanner, Tony. *City of Words: American Fiction, 1950–1970*. New York: Harper and
 Row, 1971.

Towers, Robert. "Low-Rent Tragedies." *New York Review of Books* 38.8 (May 14,
 1981): 37–40.

Troyat, Henri. *Chekov*. Trans. Michael Heim. New York: Dutton, 1986.

Vander Weele, Michael. "Raymond Carver and the Language of Desire." *Denver
 Quarterly* 22.1 (Summer 1987): 108–22.

Verley, Claudine. " 'Errand,' ou le réalisme de R. Carver dans un bouchon de
 champagne." *La nouvelle de langue anglaise* 7 (1991): 43–61.

——. "Narration and Interiority in Raymond Carver's 'Where I'm Calling From.' " *Journal of the Short Story in English* 13 (Autumn 1989): 91–102.

——. "The Window and the Eye in Carver's 'Boxes.'" *Journal of the Short Story in English* 15 (Autumn 1990): 95–106.

Wellek and Warren. *Theory of Literature.* New York: Harcourt Brace, 1956.

Wolff, Tobias. "Raymond Carver Had His Cake and Ate It Too." *Esquire* 112.3 (September 1989): 240ff.

Wood, Michael. "Stories Full of Edges and Silences." *New York Times Book Review,* April 26, 1981.

Yardley, Jonathan. "Raymond Carver's American Dreamers." *Washington Post Book World,* May 15, 1988: 3.

Young, Philip. *Three Bags Full: Essays in American Fiction.* New York: Harcourt Brace Jovanovich, 1972.

Index

A Note about the Author

Kirk Nesset is a novelist, short story writer, poet, essayist, and Assistant Professor of English and Writer-in-Residence at Whittier College. He is the father of an eleven-year-old daughter, Vanessa.

About the Type

This book is set in Joanna, a typeface designed by Eric Gill in 1930 and produced by Monotype in 1937 for machine composition. Gill lived during the years 1882–1940. He earned a reputation as a renowned stone carver, illustrator, writer, and designer. Gill is also credited with the creation of the typefaces Gill Sans and Perpetua. The typeface Joanna was named in honor of Gill's daughter, Joan. The italic version has a slope of only three degrees and was made available in 1931.